F

IN

History

THE BEST TEST PAPER BLUNDERS

Richard Benson

summersdale

F IN HISTORY

Summersdale Publishers Ltd
46 West Street
Chichester
West Sussex
PO19 1RP
UK

www.summersdale.com

Printed and bound in China

ISBN: 978-1-84953-326-3

Substantial discounts on bulk quantities of Summersdale books are available to corporations, professional associations and other organisations. For details telephone Summersdale Publishers on (+44-1243-771107), fax (+44-1243-786300) or email (nicky@summersdale.com).

Contents

Introduction

Do you remember the Dark Ages? No, not your school days but the subject of many dreary History lessons? Thousands of people have relived their exam-day nightmares with *F in Exams*, and we just couldn't resist bringing you some more hilarious test paper blunders in this bite-size History edition.

This book is full to the brim with funny answers from clueless but canny students of history which will have you cackling over Kings, hooting at invading hordes and wheezing at the World Wars! Just don't blame us if your History teacher puts you in the stocks…

Subject: **Major Conflicts**

What was the Kellogg-Briand pact?

Mr Briand had to agree not to
make cereal anymore because
Mr Kellogg didn't like the competition

Name three members of the League of Nations.

Arsenal, AC Milan and Bayern.

How might the outcome of Hitler and Chamberlain's meeting at Bad Godesberg have been improved?

It could've been held at Good Godesberg

What was the issue with the League of Nations' Secretariat?

SHE WAS RUBBISH AT FILING.

Why did the British public want more Dreadnoughts?

To balance out the Deadcrosses

Major Conflicts

What is the significance of the 1889 German Navy Cabinet?

It had brass handles and a false bottom.

What was the armistice?

It's similar to legistice, but for arms.

Name two causes of the Cold War.

1. Soldiers with runny noses.
2. Soldiers with coughs.

What was the U2 incident?

The Edge stole Bono's sunglasses.

Major Conflicts

What was the cause of the Hungarian Revolution in 1956?

THEY WERE GETTING HUNGARIER AND HUNGARIER

What was the Truman Doctrine?

A more trustworthy version of the Falseman Doctrine.

What do the letters NATO stand for?

Not At The Office

What problem rocked the USSR in 1986?

The Beatles

Major Conflicts

What is hyperinflation?

*When a bouncy castle is blown up so much
if you jumped on it, it would burst*

Give an example of semi-successful propaganda.

The only way is Essex.

Who were the members of the Big Three?

King Kong, Godzilla and
The Hulk.

What is Appel Quay famous for?

Opening Appel Door.

Give a brief summary of events of the Beagle
Conflict.

Many Beagles lost their
lives.

What was the cause of the Gallic Wars?

A gallic bread shortage.

Provide a summary of the events of the Boston Tea Party.

Everyone had a cup of tea and some cake.

Major Conflicts

What makes the 5 November a significant date in history?

The rhyme tells us to remember it.

What was the cause of the Boxer Rebellion?

The Boxers weren't being paid enough.

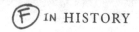

What were the terms of the Treaty of Versailles?

AUTUMN TERM, SPRING TERM,
SUMMER TERM

What happens when a country demilitarises?

Its citizens lose
motivation and feel low.

Why was the 'Glorious' Revolution of 1688 called such?

Because it was just fabulous, darling.

What was the Crimean War?

A war against criminals.

Subject: **Kings and Queens**

What is an interregnum?

A small snack between meals.

In regards to Henry VIII, what is the rhyme 'divorced, beheaded, died, divorced, beheaded, survived' about?

Death, divorce and survival.

How did William the Conqueror get his moniker?

He went to the opticians.

Name two advantages Oliver Cromwell's New
Model Army had over Charles I's Royalists.

*They were plastic so
they never got hurt.*

What was the purpose of the Domesday Book?

*People in olden times were quite
superstitions and they would
predict the end of the world.*

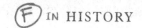

Provide two names that Elizabeth I was known by.

'Your Majesty' and
'Please Don't Cut My Head Off.'

What was the role of the Lord Protector?

Protecting the Lord

What was the War of the Roses regarding?

Trying to stop the greenfly eating them.

For what reason was James I also known as James VI?

They couldn't count.

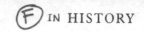

Name two attributed qualities of Richard the Lionheart.

He had long flowing hair and sharp teeth.

What was Harold II defending in the Battle of Hastings?

Hastings.

Kings and Queens

How did King Cnut reprove his courtiers?

He cnutted them.

Who were the Princes in the Tower?

Rapunzel and Sleeping Beauty are two Princes that lived in a tower.

Name one great achievement of Charlemagne.

Inventing sparkling wine.

For what reason did Boadicea revolt against the Romans?

THEY KEPT PRONOUNCING HER NAME WRONG

What was Hugh Despenser's place in the court of Edward II?

Giving out snacks and cold drinks.

What was the House of Tudor?

It had a white front with black beams and low doors.

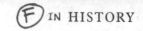

How did Mary I get the nickname 'Bloody Mary'?

From the drink.

Against who did Robert the Bruce defend Scotland?

Macbeth.

Why was James II known as the Great Pretender?

He was the most talented member of the Pretenders.

Who was Anne of Cleves?

A German lady with a big knife.

Why was George IV called the 'first gentleman of England'?

He always put the toilet seat down.

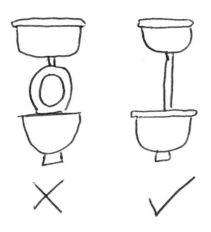

Kings and Queens

What was the Crystal Palace?

Football Team

Why was the Assembly of the Notables formed?

It was a minute-taking society.

Subject: *Twentieth Century History*

Name the five Giants of Poverty.

Jolly Green Giant, BFG, Hagrid, Beanstalk Giant & Gulliver.

What was the agreement made through the Lib-Lab pact of 1903?

People could wear flip-flops to work.

What was the subject of the Beveridge report?

Hot drinks

What, or who, were the Suffragettes?

60's pop group.

Where were the effects of the Depression least felt?

At the top of mountains.

Give a brief description of the 'never-never'.

Where Peter Pan lives.

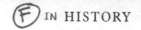

What is public health?

Anything involving eating apples outdoors or running in parks.

What is a census?

Latin for a hundred.

What happened to heavy industries during the Depression?

They got heavier, as people eat when depressed.

What was the Special Areas Act?

Something very rude.

What was the purpose of the labour exchange?

So people could try each other's jobs for a while.

Give a consequence of the General Strike.

There were no Generals to run the army.

Give a brief description of the events of 'Red Friday'.

It followed 'Really Sunny But No Sun Cream Thursday'.

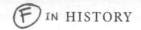

What is Social Engineering?

Inventions like Facebook and Twitter.

What caused the fall of the Berlin Wall in 1989?

Shoddy Pointing.

What was said to be the last defence against extreme poverty?

Winning the lottery.

What were the consequences of the 1765 Stamp Act?

Fair postage for all.

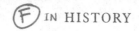

What was the Belle Epoque period?

Before Bella met Edward or
Jacob there was a time
she dated Epoque

How did the flying shuttle revolutionise the textile industry?

They could use new materials from space.

What was the Wall Street Crash?

A CAR MOUNTED THE PAVEMENT & HIT THE WALL

What is another name for the 'Roaring Twenties'?

The shouting Post-Teens.

Give a definition of a co-operative society.

A VILLAGE OF PEOPLE THAT
LIKE TO SHOP AT THEIR LOCAL
STORE.

Define the proto-industrialisation movement.

A project to create factories built
by microbes.

What sort of engine was the table engine?

It keeps your food warm.

ZOOM!

What is the poverty line?

It goes round the middle of the earth.

What were the events leading up to the St Valentine's Day Massacre?

Someone didn't get any cards.

Subject: **General History**

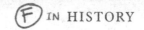

Name the four humours of Greek medicine.

Slapstick, irony, wordplay and poo jokes.

In Ancient Greece, where did the clinical observation of a patient with an illness begin?

At the doctor's

What was Vegetius famous for?

His healthy diet.

In Medieval England, what was a reredorter?

Someone who comes in to
decorate after the first time goes
wrong.

What is meant by the term 'prehistoric'?

Before anyone cared
enough to write it down.

What is the Hippocratic Oath?

An oath you don't intend to keep.

What is the 'Ides of March' famous for?

Unusual patterns in the March seas

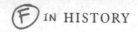

What is the definition of a 'quack' doctor?

One that specialises in ducks.

Who was the Ancient Egyptian God of Death?

A newbie.

Who were the visigoths?

Fans of The Cure in hi-vis vests.

Imsety, Hapy and Duamutef are examples of what?

The seven dwarfs.

List three notable features of Gaulish society.

Asterix, Obelix and
Cacofonix.

What language did the Romans write in?

Roman.

What was the significance of Hadrian's Wall?

It was the first ever wall.

What did an Ancient Egyptian embalmer do?

Embalmed Ancient Egyptians.

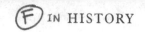

Name one characteristic of the Enlightenement.

Brightness.

Describe an Ionic column.

A column that's deliberately contrary to its expected meaning.

Describe an amphitheatre.

A place where frogs hold plays

What technological advances did Rome bring to Britain?

Roman candles.

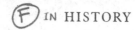

What are Picts an example of?

A tool for mining.

What is the Upper Palaeolithic?

A dinosaur's thigh bone.

Give an example of Megafauna.

A giant beby deer.

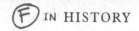

Why is the Early Stone Age contemporaneous with the Lower Palaeolithic?

They just don't get on well together.

What were flintknappers?

They stole flint and demanded a ransom for its safe return.

Define carbon dating.

It's how scientists work out the age of carbon.

What contributed to the Bronze Age collapse?

Rust.

Subject: **Politics**

What were the events of the Fashoda Crisis?

Lots of people turned up to a party in the same dress.

What was the Easter Rising?

The tradition of cooking Hot Cross Buns for Easter.

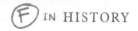

Why was Spinning Jenny phased out?

She got dizzy.

What were the Swing Rioters of 1830 protesting against?

Jazz.

Give a brief description of the Rump
Parliament.

It was held inside the
Trousers of Commons.

What was the purpose of the Barebones
Parliament?

They provide a skeleton staff When other
politicians are on holiday.

What was the position of the Whigs in the 18th Century?

On top of bald people's heads.

Politics

What factors contributed to the fall of the British Empire?

Everybody got bored of eating fish and chips all the time.

What was the Lytton Commission reporting on?

Picking up rubbish

What was Britain's interest in the Suez Canal?

That's where Suez pudding comes from.

What was known as the Pax Britannica?

British sanitary products.

Politics

Give a brief description of the Malthusian Trap theory.

You put cheese in the trap.

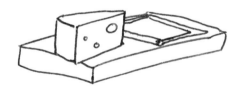

For what is the Order of the Garter awarded?

Holding up stockings.

Why were the Corn Laws repealed?

When they were pealed the
first time there were bits
left on them.

What was Chamberlain's plan for appeasement?

That peas should be
served alongside fish
and chips.

What event occurred under the Elementary
Education Act of 1870?

Sherlock Holmes became
required reading in Schools

Name two Dissenting groups.

SUGAR AND GRAVY CUBES
BOTH DISSENT IN WATER

What were the reasons for the March of the Blanketeers?

They were poor and couldn't afford duvets.

How is a polytheistic society different to a monotheistic society?

They use better filling in their walls.

Why was the Pains and Penalties Bill introduced in 1820?

To standardise footballing laws.

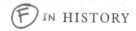

What was the Poor Law Act of 1388?

It made it illegal to be poor.

What is the definition of an Oligarchy?

A Society where ugly people are in charge.

Politics

To what extent to you agree that the Speenhamland System helped mitigate rural poverty?

They sold more pigs.

Name one of the main principles behind Chartism.

It's an unreasonable fear of charts.

If you're interested in finding out more about our humour books, follow us on Twitter:
@SummersdaleLOL

www.summersdale.com